W9-BPO-652

The Library of Disease-Causing Organisms™

FUNGI AND MOLDS

Jennifer Viegas

The Rosen Publishing Group, Inc.
New York

Published in 2004 by The Rosen Publishing Group, Inc.
29 East 21st Street, New York, NY 10010

First Edition

Library of Congress Cataloging-in-Publication Data

Viegas, Jennifer.
Fungi and molds/Jennifer Viegas.
    v. cm.—(Germs: The library of disease-
causing organisms)
Includes bibliographical references and index.
Contents: What are fungi and molds?—Symbiotes and
parasites—Fungal diseases—Preventing problems.
ISBN 0-8239-4492-1 (lib. bdg.)
1. Mycoses—Juvenile literature. [1. Fungi.
2. Molds (Fungi)]
I. Title. II. Series.
RC117.V54 2003
616.9′69—dc21

                                        2003010701

Manufactured in the United States of America

On the cover: An electron micrograph of *Candida
albicans*, the cause of candidiasis.

CONTENTS

1 What Are Fungi and Molds?

Fungi and molds have been on this planet for at least 550 million years. Dinosaurs marched over them. The first humans would have been familiar with them. It is even possible that they were some of Earth's earliest life forms. While dinosaurs died out millions of years ago, fungi and molds are still going strong.

Fungi, the plural of fungus, are nonflowering organisms that obtain food by absorption from an outside source. They often reproduce asexually, meaning without a male and female union. Fungi also possess no chlorophyll, the green, nitrogen-based substance that most plants use to convert sunlight into energy. Think of most plants that you have seen. They usually have green leaves or a green stem. Fungi do not.

Because fungi are not dependent on light, they can grow in very dark places. If you have ever explored a cave, chances are you have seen some type of fungus growing there. These organisms can even grow on the bottom of logs in a woodpile, or in a dark garden shed if the conditions are right.

The honey fungus mushrooms at left are also called bootlace mushrooms. They are parasites that grow on or around the trunks of trees, sometimes killing the trees in the process. Penicillium blue molds like the one at right often grow on fruit that has been nicked or scratched.

You have probably eaten pizza topped with sliced mushrooms. Mushrooms are nutritious and edible fungi. At the supermarket, take a minute to observe all of the different kinds of mushrooms available. Some are small and round. Others are long and dark. Mushrooms, like most fungi, come in a number of different shapes and sizes.

Mold is another type of fungus. Mold usually has a fuzzy texture and is commonly found on the surfaces of decaying food or in warm, moist places. It is often colored black, blue, green, or red. Mold often reproduces asexually, but some species do reproduce sexually by uniting two different types of cells to make what is called a zygote, the product of the cell union. Like a seed, zygotes germinate, or sprout, after a period of dormancy when the zygotes are inactive.

You do not have to look far to find mold. Undesirable forms of mold probably have, at one time, lived in your shower or bathtub. They look like dark patches living in the nooks and crannies of damp places where it is sometimes hard to clean. More desirable types of mold can be found in your local grocery store. The casing that surrounds Brie cheese is made out of mold. Roquefort and Camembert cheeses also contain certain types of mold. The mold appears in blue veins within the cheese. This is where the manufacturers injected

How to Grow Mold

Mold can be grown on a slice of bread. Simply sprinkle a few drops of water on a bread slice. Rub your index finger on a dusty surface, such as the top of an undusted television set or another piece of furniture. Rub your finger gently over the dampened bread. Cover the bread with a dish and place it in a warm area, making sure that the bread stays moist. In a few days white or black spots of mold should begin to appear on the bread. Over time the mold, which feeds on the bread, will reduce the bread slice to a wet paste.

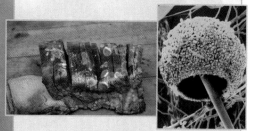

The mold at left is digesting a piece of bread and absorbing nutrients as it dissolves them. At right is an electron micrograph of a cluster of mold spores.

the mold, which breaks down the milk in the cheese to create a flavorful taste and a different texture.

Parts of a Fungus

The body of a fungus is not like the body of a human or an animal, or even like that of a plant. As humans, we are fairly compact creatures that take up a fixed amount of space. Some fungi can spread for enormous distances. A single fungus discovered in a Seattle, Washington, forest in 1992 had a structure that spread for 2.5 square miles (6.5 square kilometers). Overall, it weighed nearly 1,000 tons (1,016 metric tons). Some scientists believe it is the largest organism ever to have lived on this planet.

Although many fungi and molds are huge, they have very simple structures, especially when compared to other living organisms such as humans. Our bodies are made up of

Roquefort cheese is made from sheep's milk that has been mixed with a mold named *Penicillium roqueforti*. The cheese is aged in specially ventilated caves in France to allow the mold to grow.

many different parts and organs. We have hands, feet, legs, arms, a heart, a brain, and more. Fungi possess only four main parts: hyphae, mycelium, a fruiting body, and spores.

Hyphae

The body of a fungus actually is made up of tiny, hair-like strands called hyphae. These strands can be very thin and difficult to see without using a microscope.

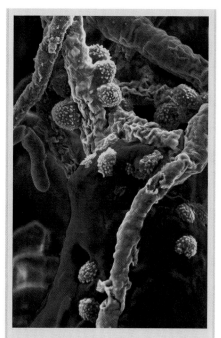

An electron micrograph of a fungal mold enlarged 1,000 times shows its threadlike hyphae. Besides keeping a fungus alive, hyphae also help bind soil particles together.

Some species of fungus have hyphae so tiny that it takes 50,000 of them laid together to make one inch. The huge Seattle fungus was not one sprawling, visible mass lying on the ground. Most of it would have been invisible to passers-by. That is because most of the hyphae were underground.

The hyphae comprise the body of the fungus. Whether above or underground, hyphae spread out in a network of twisted strands, the way roots grow. Roots, however, tend to grow in three directions—up, down, and sideways— while the hyphae of a fungus tend to spread out more in the shape of a flat mat.

Think of the hyphae like fibers in a tattered square rug. The hyphae that lie in the inner section are responsible for transporting food and water to the fungus. Because they must absorb water and nutrients, these hyphae have many small openings. The hyphae that lie on the outer edges instead are covered with protective walls. Again think of a rug, which has an edge made up of sturdy, tough fibers.

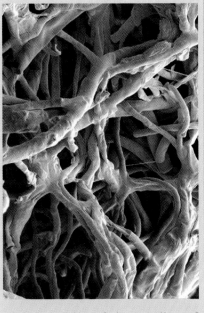

A close up view of the mycelium of *Penicillium roqueforti*. When two mycelia of the same species meet and are sexually compatible, they join together and exchange cell nuclei. This process is called diploidization.

Mycelium

Just as individual fibers put together make up a rug, individual hypha (singular for hyphae) put together make up a mycelium. "Mycelium" is a term used to describe the entire mat of tangled hyphae fibers.

Since the hyphae carry food and water to the fungus, and a fungus does not need light, the mycelium functions like the roots, stems, and leaves of a plant.

The mycelium enables a fungus to spread to other areas. If you have ever worked in the garden, you might have helped someone to separate plants that grow together. For many species, the plant can be broken off, with roots attached, and planted in another spot where it will grow into a whole new plant. The same is true for many fungi. For these species, a patch of the mycelium can be broken off and placed in a new area where it will grow into another fungus. Commercial growers of mushrooms often use this technique to increase their yield.

Fruiting Bodies and Spores

Mushrooms are one example of a fruiting body. You might think that a mushroom is an entire fungus, but it is only one small part of the entire growth. Underneath mushrooms are the hyphae and mycelium, the parts that really make up the body of the fungus. The mushroom serves as a fruit of the fungus. Just as a single apple is only one small part of a big tree, a single mushroom is only one fruiting body of a fungus.

It is incredible to think how big an average garden fungus grows. When outside, look for mushrooms. Do not pick or eat any! A number of mushrooms growing

Most *Amanita* mushrooms, like this one, are toxic, but a few, such as *Amanita caesarea, Amanita hemibapha,* and *Amanita jacksonii* are edible. Some poisonous *Amanitas* are called death angels or death caps. Because it can be difficult to tell poisonous and nonpoisonous mushrooms apart, many people get sick each year from trying wild mushrooms—and some even die.

in the wild are very poisonous. Observe how they grow. Sometimes they can be found growing in a circle, or in clusters. Now visualize that these fruiting bodies are attached to hyphae and mycelium that could radiate for miles around where the mushroom was found.

Just as fruit often contains seeds, fruiting bodies contain spores that are like the seeds of the fungus. When dropped in an appropriate environment, the spores can develop into new fungi. Fruiting bodies may produce tens of thousands of spores. Some fungi are able to shoot them out like a water pistol.

In a mushroom, spores are produced by the gills, which are the thin folds found underneath the cap. The cap is the part of the mushroom that looks like the top of an umbrella. A stalk holds up the cap and the gills. It is not easy to see the spores contained within the gills, but try placing a cap on a white paper towel under a cup. Leave it there overnight. In the morning when you pick up the cap, you should see tiny specks on the paper towel. These are the spores.

Other Types of Fungi and Molds

There are many different types of fungi. Just as mold is a type of fungus that includes numerous species, yeasts and slime molds are two other types of fungi. Yeast is a microscopic, single-celled fungus. It exists in the wild, growing on plants and in soil. Certain kinds also are cultivated in a factory setting for use in making bread, wine, beer, and other foods and drinks. Yeast feeds on sugar, nitrogen, minerals, and water. When making bread, yeast is fed a small amount of one or more of these things in a process called proofing. As the yeast feeds, it gives off carbon dioxide gas. When bread is baked, the gas is trapped in little holes around the dough, which makes the bread rise into a fluffy loaf.

Much less appetizing are slime molds, multicellular organisms that form fruiting bodies. Scientists often

Fuligo septica, or scrambled egg slime mold, appears throughout North America in cool weather, usually on decayed wood and bark mulch. However, it may also be found on compost, live plants, and lawns. It has the largest fruiting body of any of the slime molds. This mold has many common names, including dog vomit slime, troll butter, flowers of tan, and flowers of sulphur.

classify them in their own category, as they look and function somewhat differently than most molds. As the name suggests, slime mold is slimy in texture. Special cells enable it to move along a surface as it absorbs water and nutrients. When the surface dries out, the slime changes into a bunch of fruiting bodies that produce and disperse spores. If the spores land on a suitably moist surface, a new slime mold will develop.

Symbiotes and Parasites

Some trees and mushrooms live together in harmony. Take a look near the roots of a tree on a day not long after a rain shower. You might find mushrooms living there. The mushrooms benefit the tree by providing it with water and minerals, which the mushrooms absorb from the soil. The tree, in turn, might provide additional food for the mushrooms. Such happy tree-mushroom relationships often are found near the seashore, where there is sandy dirt, or in other areas where the soil quality is poor. Since the trees and mushrooms cannot exist well on their own under these circumstances, they rely on each other for survival.

Another example of beneficial fungi is the fungus gardens located in the nests of leaf-cutting ants. The ants farm a fungus garden in their colonies. Ants bring leaves to their nests, upon which a fungus grows. The leaves feed the fungus, and the fungus feeds the ants. Some fungi live on decaying matter. These are called saprophytes. Without saprophytes most organic materials would not break down properly.

Pleurotus ostreatus, or the oyster mushroom, is an edible mushroom found in temperate climates, almost always on dead trees. It can also be cultivated and so is often found in supermarkets. In the wild it is generally gathered during the fall months.

Saprophytes function like a garbage disposal, breaking down dead matter so that it can be recycled in nature. A slice of bread covered with mold that is lying on the ground, for example, will eventually turn into a pasty substance. Green plants can then absorb minerals from the bread paste. Fungi that live on living plants or animals are called parasites. Parasites nourish themselves from the host plant or animal, and do not always provide anything back in return. Many of these kinds of fungi can be harmful, such as mildew.

Mildew

Mildew refers to a number of different parasitic fungi that attack plants and things, such as books, made out of plant or animal products. Books are made out of paper, which is made out of tree pulp. Mildew feeds off of the pulp.

While the words "mildew" and "mold" sometimes are used interchangeably, mold usually has a strong color to it, while mildew generally ranges from white to off-white. Like mold, mildew grows in damp places. There are many kinds of mildew. Two major types are powdery mildew and downy mildew.

You may have seen powdery mildew on old fruit or vegetables. The visible white blotches actually are the hyphae of the fungus. The hyphae branch out across the plant to absorb its nutrients. Often, in the process of feeding on the plant, the mildew will kill the sections

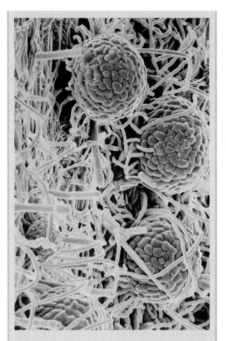

This is an electron micrograph of the hyphae of a powdery mildew. Besides affecting fruit, this mildew also infects and kills wheat and corn crops. It grows in cool and humid weather.

Irish peasants loot potatoes from a store. Potatoes became the major food crop of Irish farmers during the nineteenth century. When the farmers lost most of their potato crops to a downy mildew during the Irish Potato Famine of 1845 to 1849, hundreds of thousands of people starved or were forced to emigrate.

that it has fed on. An apple covered with mildew, for example, could eventually rot even while still on the tree. Other plants commonly affected by powdery mildew include cherries, gooseberries, grapes, peaches, peas, and roses.

Downy mildew frequently is visible as yellow splotches on the surface of leaves or fruits. As the mildew feeds, it produces sporelike structures on the bottom of the leaves, which in turn may produce even more spores. When these spores grow and develop, they send out hyphae that can extend into the interior portions of the plant. The plant becomes infected with the fungi and may die, unless the mildew is controlled.

One of the worst epidemics of downy mildew occurred between the years 1845 and 1849 in Ireland. The people in Ireland at that time were very dependent on potatoes. A species of downy mildew spread throughout the crops and killed most of the potatoes. The resulting famine killed thousands of people and forced many others to leave the country.

Mycotoxins

Some fungi produce poisonous chemicals as they feed. These chemicals are called mycotoxins. The term comes from *myco*, the Greek word for fungus. As some fungi feed on animals, plants, or items made from animal or plant materials, they secrete substances that help the fungi to absorb nutrients. In humans, our digestive enzymes are located internally in our saliva, stomachs, and intestinal tracts. Fungi do not have a stomach, so they must prepare their food for consumption outside of their bodies. The chemicals that they release to do this can be poisonous to plants and humans and animals.

Mycotoxins can form on moldy foods, especially peanuts, corn, rice, and wheat. People or animals that consume these affected foods can become sick. Sometimes livestock fed contaminated grains can then sicken humans who consume meat and dairy products made from the same livestock. Aflatoxin is the most common kind of mycotoxin. It is extremely dangerous. Studies show that it is one of the strongest cancer-causing agents yet to be identified. Two other mycotoxins are trichothecene and zearalenone. They can damage the intestines and other parts of the body when consumed.

Some studies now suggest that even inhaling mycotoxins can make a person ill. A black mold called *Stachybotrys chartarum*, commonly found on damp drywall, has been found to produce mycotoxins that are harmful when inhaled.

Stachybotrys, or black mold, has been blamed for respiratory problems when it grows in houses or office buildings. Once it begins to grow, it can be very difficult to eradicate.

Breeding Grounds for Mold and Mildew

Because mold and mildew need water to survive, they flourish in damp places. Sometimes these areas may also be dark, as the darkness prohibits light from adequately evaporating water. Such places can be found on or near indoor or outdoor plants. They may also be found inside buildings, schools, homes, cars, and any other place with inviting dampness for mold and mildew.

Watch out for the Washing Machine

Washing machines and dryers might seem to be the least likely suspects for mold havens, but fungi can collect on or near them. That is because both machines involve moisture and warmth. When clothes go in the dryer, moist, warm air is released out the back vent as the clothes dry. If the vent does not fit properly or has a hole in it, moisture can collect and attract mold and mildew. For a washing machine, water travels in and out through hoses. If these hoses have a leak, major fungi problems develop. Sometimes water near a washing machine will seep through the adjoining wall, which could cause the dangerous Stachybotrys chartarum black mold to grow.

Because of their many different water sources, such as the shower, bathtub, sink, and toilet, bathrooms often attract mold and mildew. These fungi are commonly found in the corners of the shower and in the surrounding caulk and grout. The ceiling above a shower also tends to attract mold and mildew since warm, moist air from the shower is not as dense as the surrounding air, and rises. Tiny droplets of water within the air condense on the ceiling, making a perfect breeding ground for fungi.

Even ordinary bathroom items can provide food for mold. Wallpaper, like books, is often made out of tree pulp. Since mold feeds on this plant material, the wallpaper can be home to any number of fungi. Anything organic, in this case, meaning things that contain plant or animal materials, can harbor mold. This can include paint resins on the bathroom walls, body powder, and even soap residue, as soap is made out of vegetable or animal fats.

Carpeting in the bathroom and other areas of a house or building can be like a jungle for fungi. Dampness and dirt are the biggest culprits. In carpeting, fungal food could be ground-up dirt, human or pet dander, hair, spilled food, dust mites, and anything else that may find its way into the carpeting. Mold often grows near the bottom of the carpet fiber strands, as this is where the organic material settles. However, some new carpets, when viewed under a microscope, have shown evidence of mold hyphae and spores intertwined around the uppermost carpet fibers. Some

Places in the home with lots of moisture, like this seam in the tiles of a shower, are perfect places for mildews and molds to grow.

organic matter must have landed on top of the rug. Mold began to grow even before the fungi food had a chance to settle to the carpet's bottom.

Mold can also reside in central heating and cooling systems. From there it can spread through air vents to other parts of a building. Central air-conditioning systems are some of the worst culprits. Most air conditioners work by blowing air over a cold coil. Depending on the humidity, warm air containing tiny amounts of moisture hits the cold coil. Like the ceiling over a shower, water in the air condenses. For air conditioners, the water usually is collected into a pan below the unit. Even though air conditioners create cool air, they emit heat. Dust can accumulate from the air blowing in. The combination of water, dust, and warmth can be a perfect home for fungi.

Automobiles and other vehicles can have similar problems. Like buildings, they too may contain heating and cooling systems and carpeting. Water from outside, in the air, or from the engine area can leak into the car's interior, adding to the warm, damp conditions that fungi desire. Mats and carpeting in the car, and also the seat covers and dashboard, can have nooks and crannies that are difficult to clean. These spaces can hold organic matter that could become a fungal feast.

3 *Fungal Diseases*

There are about 100,000 plant diseases linked to fungi. Seventy percent of all major crop diseases are caused by different types of molds and fungi. These diseases not only kill plants, but also result in the loss of billions of dollars each year to farmers and others impacted by the problem.

Fungi can hurt a plant at every stage of its life cycle. A fungus can hurt seeds, seedlings, and full-grown plants. Even if the fungus does not kill a plant, it can reduce the growth rate or prevent the plant from producing healthy fruits and vegetables. Fungi may attack trees within a forest and structures made out of wood.

Rusts and smuts are two common types of fungi-caused diseases that attack plants. Parasitic rusts are recognized by their orange, red, or brown color. Rusts can infect beets, cherries, coffee trees, figs, pears, peas, and grain crops like wheat, oats, corn, and rye. Smuts produce masses of black spores and also attack grain crops. The tiny flowering parts of grasses and cereals are especially vulnerable. Wheat crops suffer millions of dollars worth of losses each year due to smut damage.

Allergies

Human illnesses caused by fungi generally are divided into three different categories: allergies, toxic reactions, and fungal infections.

At some point, most of us will experience an allergic reaction. One of the most common allergies is hay fever. Hay fever often happens during the spring or fall, the times when plants release a lot of pollen into the air. Like pollen, mold and mildew also are released into the air. On a sunny day you may even be able to see what looks like dust flying around in the air inside your home. Some of those particles are probably mold spores.

Not everyone is bothered by the presence of the spores. Many people, however, are sensitive to the proteins that make up the spores. When they breathe them in, their bodies' immune systems react, causing sneezing, runny noses, swollen

This is an electron micrograph of spores from a rust fungus that infects rose plants. Most rust fungi are very specific to their host plants and can reduce crop yields.

sinuses, headaches, and other reactions. That is why health organizations track not only the amount of pollen in the air at certain times of the year, but also the amount of mold spores.

Toxic Reactions

People and animals can suffer or even die from eating fungal toxins in poisonous mushrooms or food that

These *Amanita virosa* mushrooms are also called destroying angels. They have an unpleasant smell and are highly poisonous.

has been contaminated. Fortunately, most contaminated foods let us know that they are bad to eat because they smell or look awful. An orange covered with mold, for example, is not going to be very appetizing or healthy to eat. That is why it is important to shop carefully for fresh, uncontaminated foods in the market. Avoid those that look spoiled or rotten. Spoiled foods often attract molds and mildews.

Store-bought mushrooms, the kind you find on pizza and in other foods, are safe to eat because they are carefully grown on farms that specialize in edible mushroom varieties. There are many mushrooms in the wild, however, that are extremely poisonous. Just one tiny bite from such a mushroom's cap can lead to severe illness and even death.

Many poisonous mushrooms come from a genus called *Amanita*. It includes the deadly *Amanita virosa*, or destroying angel mushroom. It can be found in many parks and gardens, particularly during the rainy season. It looks like a common button mushroom, only with a narrower stalk and cap. Because poisonous mushrooms often look like edible fungi, it is very important to never pick a wild mushroom and eat it without the help of a trained mushroom expert.

Fungal Infections

Fungal infections, also called mycoses, are diseases caused by fungi. A fungus invades living parts of the body, which results in an infection. Only 200 of the approximately 200,000 different species of fungi infect humans. Of these, only a few dozen cause most diseases. In general, disease-causing pathogens are either considered primary pathogens or opportunistic pathogens. Primary pathogens can hurt anyone. Opportunistic fungi tend to affect people who have a weakened immune system, such as people already suffering from another disease, like cancer or AIDS.

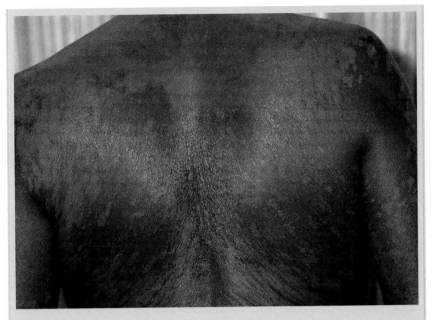

Tinea versicolor is a common skin condition caused by an overgrowth of a skin surface fungus. The fungus grows slowly and prevents the skin from tanning normally, causing pale spots. In tropical countries with continuous high heat and high humidity, people can have these spots year round. In other climates, the spots generally fade in the cooler and drier months of the year.

Fungal infections are grouped into four categories, depending on the extent of the disease and what part of the body they impact. The four groups are superficial mycoses, cutaneous mycoses, subcutaneous mycoses, and systemic mycoses.

Superficial Mycoses

Superficial mycoses are fungal infections of the hair and the outermost surface of the skin. While not life threatening, they can cause discomfort. Most of these infections occur in tropical regions throughout the world where the weather is frequently warm and conditions are moist and humid.

One such infection, Tinea versicolor, is caused by uncontrolled growth of a fungus that is commonly present on human skin in small amounts. A little bit of the fungus causes no symptoms, but when it gets out of hand, an infected person may develop scaly patches on the skin that can develop into sores. Antifungal creams usually kill the excess fungi and get rid of the problem.

Tinea nigra is another superficial mycoses. It is caused by a fungus that usually infects the feet and the palms of the hands. These areas tend to release a lot of moisture. Think about when you have been active for a while, perhaps exercising, hiking, or performing some other activity where you must move around a lot. When you remove your shoes, your feet may feel warm and moist. If you do not change your socks and bathe your feet, both the socks and your feet could become a perfect breeding ground for a fungus. Warm, moist conditions also can lead to an infection called athlete's foot, which is a cutaneous mycoses.

Cutaneous Mycoses

Fungal infections that fall under this heading affect more layers of the skin than a superficial infection. That means they go deeper than just the skin's outer surface. Cutaneous mycoses still are not life threatening but can worsen and become chronic, or long-term, if left untreated.

Athlete's foot is by far the most common cutaneous mycoses. You may have even had it yourself or know of someone who did. A fungus that attacks the feet causes it. Usually athlete's foot spreads when a person steps on a surface that has been infected with the fungus, such as a shower floor.

Symptoms of athlete's foot include itching and the development of small blisters filled with fluid on the feet. Skin around these areas can begin to crack, itch, and peel. While that in itself can cause discomfort, the small openings in the skin can allow other germs to enter, creating a much worse problem. While medicinal creams treat the condition, it sometimes takes a while, and it can easily be contracted again if you are not careful.

The term "athlete's foot" comes from the fact that many athletes get the fungus. That is because they are often walking, running, jumping, and otherwise

Foot Health

Our feet take a lot of abuse during the day, considering that they must walk over hard surfaces, wear shoes that do not always fit right, and sometimes endure sweaty socks. Take time to pamper your feet. Choose shoes and socks carefully. Make sure that you have the correct size and that socks are roomy enough to allow for some air circulation. When bathing, pay special attention to the areas between your toes and around your toenails. Fungi like these areas because they tend to be especially warm and moist. After bathing, carefully dry off your feet. If desired, use a foot powder or lotion to guard against wet, damp conditions that bacteria and fungi tend to thrive in.

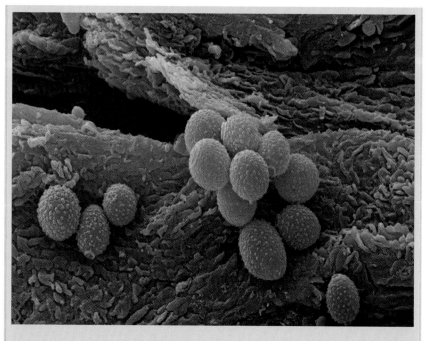

An electron micrograph of athlete's foot fungal spores (*Tinea unguium*) on a human nail. Athlete's foot can go dormant and then recur when conditions are right for it to grow. Athlete's foot can cause blisters, scaly skin, or thickened and discolored toenails.

using their feet, which causes the feet to release moisture. The moisture has a hard time evaporating inside warm tennis shoes and other sports shoes. Then the athletes often share showers and locker rooms, where the fungus can easily spread.

Candida is another common fungal infection of the skin. It is caused by an overgrowth of yeast that everyone has in small amounts in the nose, mouth, and other areas. As the yeast feeds on the skin, it can damage it, causing lesions and pus-filled infections. Candida may become quite serious if left untreated, as it can spread beyond the skin and into other parts of the body. For all fungal diseases it is important to

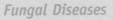

get early treatment before a minor problem develops into something much more serious.

Subcutaneous Mycoses

"Subcutaneous" means "below the skin," so subcutaneous mycoses are fungal infections that can affect the skin, tissues below the skin, and bones. Usually the fungi that cause these conditions live in soil and on decaying vegetation. Victims contract the fungus through an injury, such as walking barefoot on contaminated soil and cutting the bottom of a foot on something sharp, like the edge of a rock.

These kinds of infections are more common in tropical and subtropical areas, such as India, Africa, and Latin America. People who work outdoors, like farmers, gardeners, and nursery workers, are at greatest risk. Even if you do not know such a person directly, you may have drunk tea or coffee grown in a tropical or subtropical region. Some buyers of these products in the United States and in other countries are trying to improve the conditions of the farming communities, which hopefully will help prevent fungal infections and other related diseases.

Systemic Mycoses

As the word suggests, "systemic" means that the disease can affect the entire system, or body, of the victim. These fungal infections are extremely serious and require immediate medical attention.

Histoplasmosis, for example, is a systemic mycoses that can occur after a person has inhaled a fungus that grows as a mold in contaminated soil or in the droppings of certain birds and bats. The fungus can be breathed into human lungs where it may grow and multiply. Eventually the fungus can move to other parts of the body. The person might suffer for many years with the disease, developing a cough and shortness of breath. Ninety percent of all patients with advanced stages of the disease do not survive.

There are a number of other systemic fungal infections. While overall health standards continue to improve, problems such as climate change, disrupted ecosystems, and overcrowding seem to be good for certain fungi and bad for people trying to avoid fungal diseases.

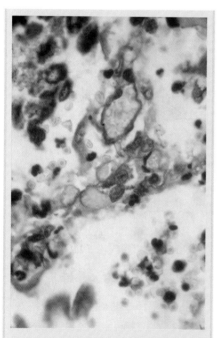

Histoplasmosis is common in the eastern and central United States. Infants, young children, older persons, and people with cancer or AIDS are the most vulnerable to this disease.

4 *Preventing Problems*

Molds and fungi are everywhere. They can live outside, in schools, in houses, in airplanes, and even in very clean places, like hospitals. It would be impossible to completely get rid of them all, and you would not want to, anyway, because many are beneficial.

Too many invasive fungi, however, can pose problems, not just because of the threat of disease, but also because molds and fungi can damage the objects that they are living on. Fungi live off of organic matter, which can exist in some surprising and unusual places. You would be amazed to learn how many materials are composed of things that used to be alive. Wood in walls can serve as food for fungi. Soap scum and dirt in the shower can be home for molds. While fungi are not smart like animals or humans because they do not have brains, they are incredibly hearty and adaptable organisms that can thrive almost anywhere. It is important to keep their numbers in check, particularly indoors.

Libraries often have problems with mold growing in books. Treating it involves using a HEPA vacuum, soft brushes, and disinfectant, as well as wiping down the book shelves and anything the books have touched.

Moldy Books

One might say that this is a moldy book because it is about molds and fungi, but books can literally harbor molds if they are not cared for properly. Perhaps you might have opened a book at a library or at a used book sale and smelled a musty odor. The odor is probably due to mildew living in or on the book. Books need to be kept dry and clean. Any kind of water or dampness can attract molds. If you accidentally drop a book or any kind of paper product in water, make sure that you allow the object to dry thoroughly. This will prevent molds from moving into the book.

Fungi at Home

Houses and apartments are cozy places for humans and pets, but they also can provide a nice haven for molds and fungi if conditions are right. Any place that is damp tends to attract fungi. Obvious places include the shower, sink, and toilet in the bathroom, and the kitchen sink. Because of its size and daily use, the shower tends to be the biggest mold target.

Be sure to clean the shower after you use it. A squeegee works well for removing excess moisture from the shower walls and the shower floor. As often as possible, spray the shower with a disinfectant cleanser and scrub it down to remove dirt and oil. Although not visible, our bodies release oil and dead skin each time we bathe. The oil can collect in the shower and attract fungi, so it is important to clean the shower just as you clean yourself.

Carpeting is one of the worst culprits for attracting molds and mildew. If the subflooring is not sealed properly, moisture can be absorbed into carpets and rugs resting on top of it. Run your hand over the carpeting to check for dampness. Even if the carpet is not damp, it can hold mold spores and support mold growth.

Be sure to vacuum the carpet regularly to prevent mold growth and the spread of spores. There are many different vacuums on the market. Some work better than others. If you have a lot of carpeting, it is worth investing in a vacuum cleaner with good suction and an airtight filtering system.

Choose the Right Cleaning Tools

Using the right tools will make cleaning easier and more effective. For vacuum cleaners, it helps to have a HEPA filter. HEPA stands for "high efficiency particulate arrestance." That is just a long-winded phrase meaning that dust and mold spores cannot easily escape the vacuum because the unit is airtight. This helps to keep the dust and mold in the vacuum bag or container. Also, look for sponges that contain a mold inhibitor. While we associate sponges with cleanliness, a damp sponge can be attractive to fungi. You may have smelled a sponge that had a bad odor to it. Even for sponges with mold inhibitors, be sure to rinse them thoroughly after use and allow them to dry out between cleanings.

Fungi on Wheels

Cars make attractive homes for fungi. Be sure to vacuum and clean any carpeting, fabric, and other places in the car that might attract molds. It is important to quickly clean up car spills before they develop into bigger problems. For example, someone might spill a milk drink in the car over the weekend. If the spill is not properly cleaned up, by the end of the following week, that area could produce a rotten smell that could spread to other areas of the car. That is because the milk spoiled and then attracted bacteria and molds to the area.

Spores in the Air

Any kind of forced air system, such as central heating or air-conditioning, can spread mold spores and fungi if not maintained properly. Do what you can to keep vents clean and dry. It then might be necessary to hire professionals to come in and take apart the unit for a more thorough cleaning. At some point, you might have seen a heating company do this. They bring in giant vacuum cleaners that are not practical for homeowners to own. Hoses attached to the vacuums can go deep into areas that you could not reach with a handheld vacuum.

Fungi in Food

Mushrooms are a rare example of a fungus that is good to eat. Mushrooms have a lot of vitamins and minerals that are both healthy and tasty to consume. For other foods, try to prevent mold and fungus by

Vacuums with HEPA filters can clean up many mold and fungi spores. On the other hand, older vacuums may just spread the spores around and make the problem worse.

Porcini mushrooms like these are prized for their rich and buttery taste and rarity. The name "porcini" is Italian for "little pig." They grow in spring and fall, and are often gathered by professional mushroom hunters.

storing them properly. Remember that molds and fungi prefer warm places. Refrigerators and freezers help to prevent fungi from growing because they keep food very cold. For foods that cannot be refrigerated, store them in airtight containers. This, too, will help to prevent fungi, because mold spores in the air will not be able to land on the food.

If There Is an Injury

At some point, all of us suffer from cuts, scrapes, bruises, and perhaps even more serious injuries. If possible, try to clean the wounded area. Dirt can hold molds and bacteria that could infect the cut. When possible, use an antifungal spray or cream to kill any germs or mold spores that might be present. Finally, cover the wound with a bandage. The bandage will promote healing and protect the injured area.

It takes a lot of work to prevent molds and fungi from developing into problems. Whether caring for an injury or cleaning your home, time and effort are required to keep fungi at bay. Develop healthy routines throughout your day to ensure that molds and fungi do not get the upper hand. You will not only safeguard your belongings, but you will also help to prevent the illnesses that fungi can cause.

Glossary

aflatoxin   A common form of mycotoxin that can cause health problems in animals and humans.

allergy   A condition where the body is sensitive to mold spores, pollen, or other substances. Exposure to them causes the immune system to react, leading to coughing, sneezing, a runny nose, and other symptoms.

chlorophyll   A green, nitrogen-based substance that most plants use to convert sunlight into energy.

cutaneous mycoses   Fungal infections of the skin.

fruiting body   The part of the fungus that carries spores and handles reproduction, such as a mushroom.

gills   The folds underneath a mushroom cap that hold spores.

hyphae   Tiny, hairlike strands that make up the body of a fungus.

mildew   A type of fungus that grows in damp places and usually is white or off-white in color.

mushroom   A fungus that is actually the fruiting body of a larger organism.

mushroom cap   The top round section of a mushroom.

mycelium The mat or body of a fungus, made up of tangled hyphae fibers.

mycoses Fungal infections.

mycotoxins Potentially dangerous substances produced by some fungi.

rust A parasitic orange, red, or brown fungal infection that appears on plants.

saprophytes Fungi that live on decaying matter.

slime molds Multicellular organisms that form fruiting bodies.

smut A type of fungal disease that produces masses of black spores and often attacks food crops.

spores Similar to seeds but containing no food for independent growth, spores are what enable fungi to spread and reproduce.

superficial mycoses Fungal infections that involve the hair or other outermost layers of the skin.

subcutaneous mycoses Fungal infections that can affect tissue below the skin's surface, along with bones.

systemic mycoses Fungal infections that can attack the entire body.

toxic reaction What happens after a person ingests a toxin, like a poisonous mushroom.

yeast A microscopic, single-celled fungus.

For More Information

Centers for Disease Control
1600 Clifton Road
Atlanta, GA 30333
(404) 639-3311
(800) 311-3435
Web site: http://www.cdc.org

Mushroom Culture magazine
Publisher: Florida Mycology Research Center
P.O. Box 18105
Pensacola, FL 32523-8105
(850) 327-4378

National Institutes of Health
9000 Rockville Pike
Bethesda, MD 20892
(301) 496-4000
e-mail: NIHinfo@od.nih.gov
Web site: http://www.nih.gov

Owl magazine
25 Boxwood Lane
Buffalo, NY 14227-2707
Web site: http://www.owlkids.com/owl

Science Made Simple magazine
P.O. Box 503
Voorhees, NJ 08043
Web site: http://www.sciencemadesimple.com

The World Health Organization
Avenue Appia 20
1211 Geneva 27
Switzerland
Web site: http://www.who.int/en

Web Sites

Due to the changing nature of Internet links, the Rosen Publishing Group, Inc., has developed an online list of Web sites related to the subject of this book. This site is updated regularly. Please use this link to access the list:

http://www.rosenlinks.com/germ/fumo

For Further Reading

Arora, David. *All That the Rain Promises and More: A Hip Pocket Guide to Western Mushrooms.* Berkeley, CA: Ten Speed Press, 1990.

Arora, David. *Mushrooms Demystified: A Comprehensive Guide to the Fleshy Fungi.* Berkeley, CA: Ten Speed Press, 1986.

Fowler, Allan. *Good Mushrooms and Bad Toadstools.* New York: Scholastic Library Publishing, 1998.

Grafton, Carol Belanger. *The Romance of the Fungus World: An Account of Fungus Life in Its Numerous Guises, Both Real and Imaginary.* Mineola, NY: Dover Publications Inc., 1997.

Hudler, George W. *Magical Mushrooms, Mischievous Molds.* Princeton, NJ: Princeton University Press, 2000.

Lincoff, Gary A. *National Audubon Society Field Guide to North American Mushrooms.* New York: Alfred A. Knopf, 1981.

Little, Charles E. *Dying of the Trees: The Pandemic in America's Forests.* New York: Viking Penguin, 1997.

Pascoe, Elaine. *Slime Molds and Fungi.* Stamford, CT: Gale Group, 1998.

Bibliography

Brodie, Harold J. *Fungi: Delight of Curiosity*.
Toronto: University of Toronto Press, 1978.

Drexler, Madeline. *Secret Agents: The Menace of
Emerging Infections*. Washington, DC: Joseph
Henry Press, 2002.

Froman, Robert. *Mushrooms and Molds*. New
York: Thomas Y. Crowell Company, 1972.

Griffith, H. Winter. *Complete Guide to Symptoms,
Illness & Injury*. New York: The Berkley
Publishing Group, 1995.

May, Jeffrey C. *My House Is Killing Me!*
Baltimore: The Johns Hopkins University
Press, 2001.

Sharma, Rajendra. *The Family Encyclopedia of
Health*. Boston: Element Books, Inc., 1998.

Silverstein, Alvin. *Fungi* (The Kingdoms of Life).
New York: Twenty-First Century Books, 1996.

Simon, Hilda. *Partners, Guests and Parasites*. New
York: The Viking Press, 1970.

Tesar, Jenny. *Fungi* (Our Living World).
Woodbridge, CT: Blackbirch Press,
Incorporated, 1994.

Zellerbach, Merla. *The Allergy Sourcebook*. Los
Angeles: Lowell House, 1998.

Index

About the Author

Jennifer Viegas is a reporter for Discovery News, the news service for the Discovery Channel. She also is a features columnist for Knight Ridder newspapers.

Photo Credits

Cover © Eye of Science/Photo Researchers, Inc.; pp. 1, 3, 4, 6, 14, 20, 23, 29, 33, 36, 40-48 courtesy of Public Health Image Library/Centers for Disease Control and Prevention; p. 5 (left) © Carl Schmidt-Luchs/Photo Researchers; p. 5 (right) © Clouds Hill Imaging Ltd./Corbis; p. 6 (left) © Cordelia Molloy/Photo Researchers, Inc.; pp. 6 (right), 16 © Microfield Scientific LTD/Photo Researchers, Inc.; p. 7 © Adam Woolfitt/Corbis; p. 8 © Gary D. Gaugler/Photo Researchers, Inc.; p. 9 © Andrew Syred/Photo Researchers, Inc.; p. 11 © Mike Zens/Corbis; p. 13 © Kevin Schafer/Corbis; p. 15 © Mike Zens/Corbis; p. 17 Private Collection/Bridgeman Art Library; p. 19 © Dr. Richard Kessel & Dr. Gene Shih/Visuals Unlimited; p. 21 © 1999-2003 Getty Images, Inc.; pp. 24, 30 © Science Photo Library/Photo Researchers; p. 25 © Matt Meadows/Photo Researchers; p. 27 © Logical Images/Custom Medical Stock Photo; p. 32 © OJ Staats, MD/Custom Medical Stock Photo; p. 34 © Erich Lessing/Art Resource, NY; p. 37 © Royalty Free/Corbis; p. 38 © Owen Franken/Corbis.

Designer: Thomas Forget; Editor: Jake Goldberg; Photo Researcher: Sherri Liberman